ALEXANDRA HEDIN

Entertaining at Home

::

Inspiration, recipes,
and crafts for creating
a lovely life

PHOTOGRAPHY by JEFF HOBSON

Sea Script Company
Seattle, Washington

ISBN: 978-0-9828663-1-3
Library of Congress Card Catalogue No.: 2010939585

First Printing January 2011

Printed in Canada

Sea Script
SEA SCRIPT COMPANY
www.seascriptcompany.com
206.748.0345

Dedicated to my dad, Thom Kroon, without whom I never would have made the leap.

table of contents

: :

introduction

::

I love to entertain. And not just the big parties with fancy invitations and days spent cooking. I love to entertain my husband and my children too by making them special treats, remembering special occasions and events, or just spending time crafting and cooking with them.

I believe that life should be lovely and it's the little moments that we create each day that make it so. I have been blessed with a life better than I could have imagined. I have parents who spent the better part of my childhood creating special moments for my sister and me; I have a husband who loves my crazy little ideas and indulges them completely; and I have children who are as curious and imaginative as I could have ever hoped. I live a charmed life.

And I live that charmed life in a tiny house wearing sweatpants. It's not about the possessions we have or where we live that make life lovely, but by the people we surround ourselves with and the life we choose to create.

I hope that this book will encourage to you to create a lovely life for yourself. It's as much about empowering you to create experiences and events as it is about parties and cooking.

a simple brunch
for friends

menu

::

german pancakes

berry compote

fresh fruit & sliced salami

granola & greek yogurt

lemon pannacotta with blueberry sauce

bloody mary bar

crafts

::

monogrammed ribbon napkin rings

square flower arrangement

My friends Thomas and Ken are two of the best hosts I know. Not only are they gracious and inviting, but they also have a way of making gourmet food seem simple.

Brunch is the perfect way to simply entertain a group of friends—it also removes excuses for not having friends over. Entertaining is less about creating a picture perfect event and more about spending time together. Thomas and Ken are famous for creating perfect parties every time. It's not always because the food is amazing (it is) but because they are both relaxed and their attitude is contagious. The reason they are able to stay relaxed the whole time is that they don't put a lot of stress on themselves. By using high quality ingredients, they take a simple idea—like a fresh fruit plate—and make it elegant and a little unexpected.

We decided to throw a party together for all our friends. While Thomas and Ken prepared the food, I decorated the table. A color scheme is a really easy way to make everything look pulled together. Pick colors that match your space—I used orange and blue for everything because it matched the kitchen perfectly.

It's easy to create the look yourself when you work with what you have. The only things I added to the space were flowers, giant orange dinner plates (that I used as chargers), blue napkins, and monogrammed ribbon napkin rings.

Simple square flower arrangements look modern and elegant down the center of a bare table.

TP

Ken drizzles the top of the fruit and salami plate with **truffle oil** for an elegant and delicious touch. It doesn't take much to make a **big impact.**

At each place, a **monogrammed napkin ring** is practical and charming.

german pancakes

Serves 4

My mom used to make these for weekend breakfasts because they are simple, but really impressive when they puff up. The key is making sure your pan is hot before you add the batter. This is an old family recipe we have been making so long it's almost foolproof.

1/4 cup butter
3 eggs
3/4 cup milk
3/4 cup flour
berry compote, page 10
whipped cream for garnish

Preheat the oven to 425°.

Divide butter among 4 individual ramekins (or use one large 2 to 3 quart pan). Arrange ramekins on a cookie sheet and place in a hot oven until butter melts completely and bubbles.

In a blender, beat eggs for 1 minute. With the blender still running, slowly add milk, then slowly add flour.

Pour batter into hot ramekins about halfway full. Return ramekins to the oven and bake 20 minutes or until puffy.

to serve :: Spoon berry compote into the center of each pancake and serve hot. Top with a dollop of whipped cream.

berry compote

Serves 6 to 8

This is perfect on top of a German pancake, but just as perfect on a waffle. Use fresh berries when they are in season, but frozen when they are out of season.

1 cup blueberries
1 cup raspberries
1 cup sliced strawberries
1/2 cup cointreau
1/2 cup water

Place all ingredients in a saucepan and simmer over low heat until liquid is reduced to half, about 30 minutes. Remove from heat and serve warm over pancakes, waffles, or ice cream.

fresh fruit & sliced salami

Serves 6 to 8

You can use any fruit, whatever is in season is always best. Be sure to have an assortment of flavors, textures, and colors on the plate. Presentation is everything! Buy the best salami as well. If it comes pre-sliced, I usually have serious doubts. In Seattle I always buy Salumi salami.

1/4 cantaloupe, thinly sliced
2 bunches concord grapes
1 pint strawberries, hulled
6 kiwi, peeled and sliced
1 pint bing cherries
1/4 pound mortadella
1/4 pound sopressata
1/4 pound salami
truffle oil

Arrange fruit and salami on a platter, alternating a salami between each fruit. Pile grapes and cherries in the center of the plate.

With your thumb over the top of the truffle oil bottle, slowly drizzle 1 to 2 teaspoons of oil over the entire platter. Be sure to taste to make sure your oil does not overpower the fruit!

granola & greek yogurt

Serves 6 to 8

I use a light baking syrup instead of the traditional honey because it imparts a sweeter flavor and has a better consistency. Called Lius Sirap at Scandanavian stores, it's fairly simple to find in the Seattle area. If you can't find it, replace with honey.

1/2 cup brown sugar
1/2 cup vegetable oil
1/2 cup Lius Sirap or honey
2 teaspoons vanilla
2 teaspoons cinnamon
4 cups rolled oats
2 cups sliced almonds
1/2 cup flax seeds
1/2 cup wheat germ
2 cups coconut
1/2 cup chopped dried apricots
1/2 cup dried cranberries
1/2 cup golden raisins
1/2 cup raisins
Greek yogurt

Preheat the oven to 325°.

In the bowl of a stand mixer fitted with the paddle attachment, blend together sugar, oil, syrup (or honey), vanilla, and cinnamon. Add oats and combine until well coated.

Spread the oats onto a cookie sheet and bake for 10 minutes until bubbly. Add almonds, flax seed, and wheat germ and stir to coat. Bake another 5 minutes. Mix in coconut and return to the oven for 15 minutes. Stir occasionally and watch constantly to prevent excessive browning. Remove from oven, toss with dried fruit and let cool.

When completely cool, break into pieces and store in an airtight container for up to one week. Serve with Greek yogurt and your favorite fruit.

lemon pannacotta with blueberry sauce

Makes 12 individual servings

This pannacotta is literally heaven. The combination of the tangy lemon with the flavorful blueberry sauce is refreshing and delicious. This can be made several days ahead and refrigerated. Make it when you have a few minutes and it will be so easy to impress.

vegetable oil
1 cup whole milk
1 cup whipping cream
1 teaspoon pure vanilla extract
juice from 3 lemons (about 10 tablespoons)
2 teaspoons unflavored gelatin
1/2 cup sugar
1 cup crème fraiche
zest from 3 lemons
blueberry sauce, page 18
2 kiwis, sliced into 6 rounds each

Lightly oil (spray kind works best) 6 ramekins or all 12 cups in a muffin tin. Mix together milk, cream, and vanilla in a heavy saucepan. Bring to a simmer, but don't let boil. Remove from the heat and let cool while the gelatin softens (below).

Pour lemon juice in a small bowl and sprinkle gelatin on top. Let stand 10 minutes or until the gelatin is soft.

Add the gelatin and sugar to the milk mixture in the saucepan. Stir over low heat until the sugar is dissolved. Remove from heat and quickly whisk in crème fraiche and lemon zest. Divide among ramekins or muffin tin cups and refrigerate overnight.

to serve :: Run a knife around the edge of each pannacotta and turn out onto a plate. If the bottom is sticking, place the very bottom of the ramekin in a shallow bowl with warm water for a few seconds. Top with blueberry sauce, fresh blueberries, and a slice of kiwi.

blueberry sauce

3 cups blueberries
3 tablespoons brown sugar
1/4 cup blueberry syrup (look for the Elki brand)
3 tablespoons cointreau

Purée blueberries with brown sugar, syrup, and cointreau. Strain mixture into a bowl, pressing the solids to remove all the liquid. Throw out the solids and put the sauce in a container.

bloody mary bar

4 ounces V8 juice
2 ounces pepper vodka
1 teaspoon Worcestershire sauce
pepper

In a highball glass, blend together V8, vodka, and Worcestershire. Add ice and season with pepper.

Top with your favorite garnishes. Mine include pickled beans, celery stalks, grilled shrimp, pickled asparagus, lemon and lime wedges, and green olives.

monogrammed ribbon napkin rings

Using ribbon and paint you can easily make napkin rings for a huge crowd. These tie nicely around a napkin creating a modern and fresh look on the table.

freezer paper
x-acto knife
letter stencils (optional)
2" wide grosgrain ribbon
fabric paint
craft paint brush
iron

step 1 :: Cut a small piece of freezer paper the width of the ribbon.

step 2 :: Trace monogram letters onto the paper (shiny side down) using the letter stencils

step 3 :: Cut out the letters using an x-acto knife.

step 4 :: Iron the freezer paper stencil onto the ribbon using a hot iron. Be sure the shiny side of the paper is down.

step 5 :: Using a small amount of paint, dab in the stencil with the paint brush. Do not use too much paint or it will begin to seep.

step 6 :: Allow to dry and remove the stencil.

square flower arrangement

This is my favorite last minute arrangement because it can be made with almost any flower you have on hand. The key is to keep it monochromatic and tightly packed. Several vases look lovely gathered together in a group or lined up down a table.

4" square vase
floral oasis
table knife
straight pins
large banana leaves or other long 4" wide leaves
1 bunch flowers

step 1 :: Cut oasis to fit snugly into the vase using the table knife. Allow about 1/4" clearance on all sides.

step 2 :: Wrap the perimeter of the oasis with banana leaves and secure with straight pins.

step 3 :: Place the oasis in the vase and fill the vase with water. Continue filling the vase until the oasis can no longer soak up any more liquid.

step 4 :: Begin adding flowers. Start on the outside of the vase and work in. Cut stems so the base of the flowers just touch the top of the oasis. Gather tightly together!

homemade spa party

menu

::

baked potato chips & tzaziki dip

tomato blue cheese tart

chocolate chip cookies

lemon-limeade

cucumber water

crafts

::

olive oil salt scrub

wood stamped pillows

One of my favorite ways to relax is spending a day at the spa. I don't know many people who would ever turn down a little pampering! However, it's not a cheap way to entertain and spoil your friends—unless you bring the spa home! I created a spa day for my cousin Victoria and a few of her friends to celebrate their high school graduation.

To start, I created a spa-like atmosphere on my back porch with wood stamped pillows and white umbrellas. Printing your own pillows is a simple, custom touch for any event. I made the pillowcases using plain canvas on the front and patterned canvas on the back, then stamped the plain canvas with an antique wood stamp and fabric paint. If you don't sew, you can get the same look using inexpensive pillow covers in plain colors and stamping them. I chose to use green and yellow to make the whole deck look summery and bright.

The girls began their day of pampering with spa treatments on the lawn using homemade bath bombs and salt scrubs. The girls did the treatments themselves and had a pile of colored nail polishes handy for finishing touches on their pedicures. If you don't want to do everything yourself, consider hiring a few manicurists from a local salon to come by.

A simple lunch in the sun capped off our afternoon. I used summery flavors to create our spa menu and the light choices were a satisfying end to a relaxing day.

To send the girls home in style, I bottled up the same salt scrubs and bath bombs we used for our treatments and had them waiting at the door. Now they can pamper themselves anytime.

galvanized buckets from the hardware store are an inexpensive way to soak lots of toes.

Make your own **olive oil scrub** to send home with your guests.

wood stamped pillows create a custom spa look wherever you are.

baked potato chips & tsatziki dip

Serves 4

I love having potato chips at a party—but sometimes it seems really tacky to rip open a bag. After seeing several recipes for making your own in the oven, I decided to try my hand at it. They are delicious! And even better with a tangy dip like tsatziki.

2 pounds russet potatoes, thinly sliced
4 teaspoons salt
2 teaspoons pepper
2 tablespoons olive oil

Preheat the oven to 400°.

Place the baking sheet in the oven while it warms up. Dry the potato slices with a paper towel. Toss with oil and half of the salt and pepper. Place slices on the preheated baking sheet and bake for 10 minutes. Flip slices over and bake another 5 to 10 minutes until golden brown. Remove from the oven and toss in remaining salt and pepper. Serve immediately.

tsatziki dip

8 ounces plain Greek yogurt
3" section of cucumber, peeled
1 teaspoon salt
1 teaspoon freshly ground pepper

Grate cucumber into a bowl making sure to capture any liquid created. Stir in yogurt and season with salt and pepper. Let sit, refrigerated, at least 1 hour or overnight.

tomato blue cheese tart

Serves 6 to 8

I tried several versions of savory tarts and quiche recipes before I landed on this delicious one. It has just enough blue cheese to be indulgent and is well balanced by a handful of mixed greens. It's the perfect "ladies lunch."

2 frozen deep-dish pie crusts
15 ounces whole milk ricotta cheese
6 ounces good quality blue cheese, crumbled
1/2 cup shredded parmesan cheese
2 large eggs, beaten
3 medium tomatoes, thinly sliced
salt and pepper
lemon wedges for garnish

Preheat the oven to 350˚.

Place the frozen pie crusts in the oven and bake 8 to10 minutes until brown. Remove and let cool. If bubbles form, prick the bottoms with a fork.

In a bowl, whisk together ricotta, 4 ounces of blue cheese, parmesan, and eggs until just combined. Divide the cheese mixture evenly into the pie crusts and top with tomato slices. Sprinkle the tops with the remaining blue cheese, salt, and pepper.

Bake for 20 to 25 minutes. Remove from the oven and let cool 10 minutes. Serve with your favorite blend of mixed greens and a wedge of lemon.

chocolate chip cookies

Makes 2 dozen cookies

I started making chocolate chip cookies at age 12 searching for the perfect cookie recipe. At 12, I certainly didn't have it—and almost everyone I know will attest to that. There were dozens of versions of cookies that finally led to this recipe that everyone agrees is heavenly. Can you imagine my frustration when Martha Stewart came out with her new recipe that was shockingly similar to mine? At least great minds think alike.

2 1/4 cups flour
1 teaspoon salt
1 teaspoon baking powder
1 teaspoon baking soda
1 1/2 cups butter, room temperature
1 1/2 cups brown sugar
1/2 cup sugar
2 eggs
1 teaspoon vanilla
2 cups chocolate chips

Preheat the oven to 350°.

In a small bowl, blend together dry ingredients (flour, salt, soda, and powder) and set aside. In the bowl of an electric mixer, cream together sugars and butter until pale and fluffy. Add eggs and vanilla and beat until incorporated.

Add dry ingredients to the mixer and combine on low speed until incorporated. Stir in chocolate chips.

Scoop balls of dough using an ice cream scoop or two spoons and drop onto a cookie sheet. Allow plenty of room between cookies as they may spread. Bake 10 to 12 minutes until crispy on the edges. Let cool on the cookie sheet 10 minutes, transfer to a wire rack, and let cool completely.

lemon-limeade

This summertime basic can be made at almost any time and kept in the fridge. It's always delightful to open the fridge to freshly made lemonade. And with a little iced tea, it's even better!

1 cup fresh squeezed lemon juice (about 6 lemons)
1 tablespoon lime juice (about 1 lime)
2 quarts water
1 cup sugar

In a small saucepan, simmer 1 cup water with sugar until sugar dissolves to make a simple syrup. Remove from the heat and let cool.

Squeeze the lemons and limes to extract all of the juice and pour into a pitcher. Stir in the remaining water and simple syrup. Refrigerate before serving.

cucumber water

water
ice cubes
1/2 medium cucumber

Fill a one gallon pitcher with water and ice. Slice the cucumber and place in the pitcher. Refrigerate for 1 hour. Add ice cubes before serving.

olive oil salt scrub

1 cup epsom salts
1 cup coarse ground sea salt
1 cup organic olive oil
1 tablespoon dried lavender, crushed

step 1 :: Mix all ingredients together.

step 2 :: Let sit at least 2 hours.

step 3 :: Place in jars and wrap with a bow.

note :: If you don't have lavender growing or left over from summer, you can purchase culinary grade lavender at specialty grocery stores.

wood stamped pillows

Makes 3 pillows

3 12" x 12" pieces plain canvas
3 12" x 12" pieces patterned canvas
1 wood stamp
paint
paper towels
paper plate
brayer (mini-roller)

step 1 :: Pour paint onto a paper plate.

step 2 :: Place plain canvas on top of 2 to 3 layers of paper towel. Ensure there are no wrinkles or folds in either layer.

step 3 :: Run the brayer through the paint to create an even, and not too thick, coat of paint.

step 4 :: Run the brayer across the bottom of the wood stamp to create an even, and not too thick, coat of paint.

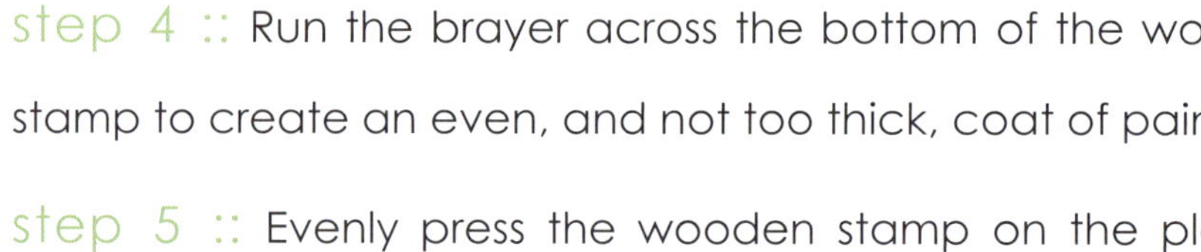

step 5 :: Evenly press the wooden stamp on the plain canvas. The paper towels are necessary to cushion the stamp (which is why rubber stamps are the modern option) and to prevent leakage onto your surface. Continue stamping until the canvas is a pattern you like and all the plain canvas is stamped.

step 6 :: With right sides together, sew the pillow together leaving a small opening at the bottom. Turn the pillow right-side-out using the small opening at the bottom.

step 7 :: Stuff with a pillow form.

step 8 :: Hand stitch the small opening at the bottom together.

a beach-y bridal shower

menu

::

gwen's crab cakes

steamed clams & mussels

smoked salmon cucumber bites

blueberry mini-tarts

marionberry martini

craft

::

shell wine glass name tags

My cousin grew up by the beach on Whidbey Island and decided to get married on the water. A bridal shower inspired by the shells and water of Puget Sound seemed only appropriate.

The wedding colors were blue and white, so I choose to keep those colors and added a splash of bright pink. It's not necessary to use the wedding colors for a shower, but to be inspired by the colors or theme of the wedding helps to personalize the event. The bright pink I chose complimented their colors and added a little pop to everything—and it made it a little bit different from the wedding.

The beautiful summer weather was perfect for hosting a cocktail party on the deck with seasonal drinks and bite-sized food. Under my outdoor umbrellas, I set a series of bar height tables topped with linens. I had a really hard time finding exactly what I wanted for colors and patterns of table linens, so I went to the fabric store and found exactly what I was looking for and hemmed it to fit the tables. On the tables, I set centerpieces of hurricane vases. Some were filled with sand, shells and a candle while others were filled with bright pink dahlias, the perfect summer flower.

For our cocktail event, I made food inspired by some of our favorite restaurants on Whidbey Island made into bite-sized pieces. Served alongside marionberry martinis made from Whidbey Island's famous marionberry crops, it was a completely Island inspired menu.

Little plates and
big bowls
of food
encourage
guests to make
several trips to
the table.

Don't forget the details! To start the event off with a bang, I sent a **pair of flip-flops** to each guest with the **invitation tied to the toe.** Packaged in a small box, everyone knew this was a party not to be missed!

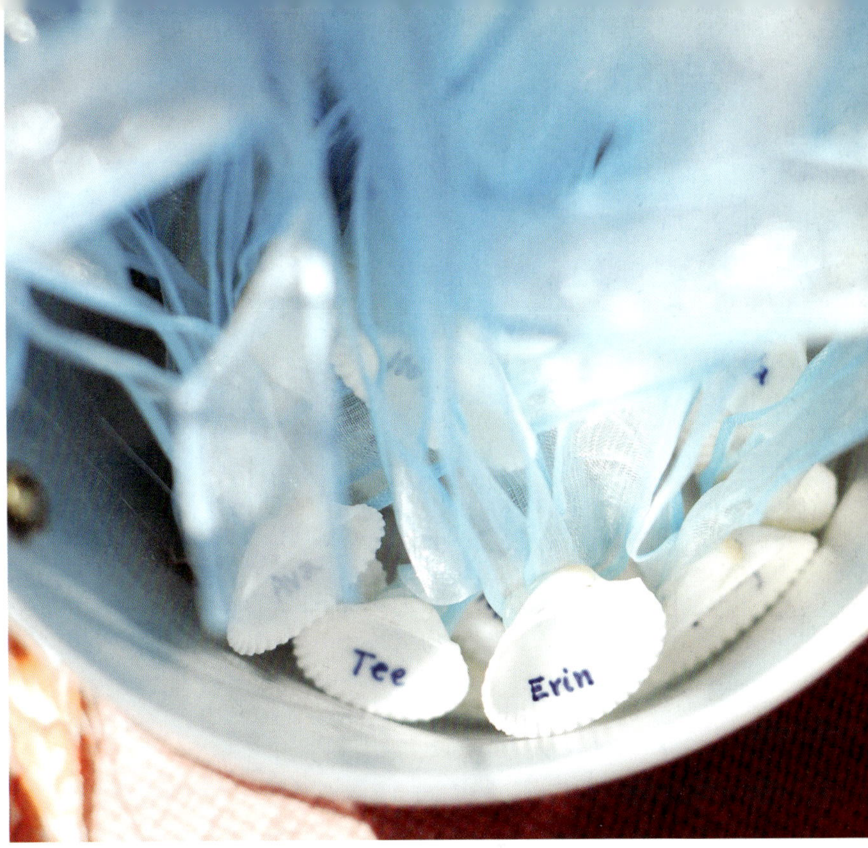

Personalized wine glass tags made from shells ensure every guest can find their glass in a very festive way.

gwen's crab cakes

Serves 4 to 6

These are my mom's specialty. Anytime there is fresh crab around we insist she makes her crab cakes. Over the past few years, she's eaten crab cakes all over the world to figure out the best way to make them full of crab, full of flavor, and not overpowered by one ingredient (unless that ingredient is crab).

1 pound fresh cracked dungeness crab
1/4 cup mayonnaise
1 egg, beaten
1 cup panko breadcrumbs
(available at Asian specialty markets)
2 tablespoons Old Bay seasoning
1/4 teaspoon dry mustard
1 teaspoon baking soda
juice of 1/2 lemon
salt and pepper
1 tablespoon butter

Mix together all ingredients, except butter, and add salt and pepper to taste. Melt the butter in a skillet over medium heat.

Form the crab mixture into patties. Place the patties in a preheated pan and cook about 3 minutes on each side until cakes are golden on all sides and warm throughout.

steamed clams & mussels

Serves 4 to 6

1 pound each, mussels and clams
1 tablespoon olive oil
2 cloves garlic, chopped
2 tablespoons basil, chopped
2 tablespoons thyme, chopped
2 scallions, greens and whites chopped
1 cup white wine
1 lemon, juiced

To prepare the shellfish, pull out the 'beard' of the mussels using needle nosed pliers. The beard is a small black piece that hangs out the flat side of the shell. It is gritty to eat, so it's necessary taking the time to pull them off.

In a deep wide bottomed pan, heat olive oil over medium heat. Add garlic and cook until fragrant (about a minute), then add herbs and scallions. Cook several minutes until scallions are limp. Add mussels and clams, wine, and lemon juice. Cover with a lid and let steam about 10 minutes until all shells are open. If any shells do not open, discard them and do not eat.

Serve hot with melted butter and bread for soaking up the juice in the pan.

smoked salmon cucumber bites

Makes 1 dozen bites

2 english cucumbers, sliced into 2" pieces
8 ounces cream cheese
2 ounces smoked salmon
2 sprigs dill, chopped (about 2 tablespoons)
dill sprigs for garnish

Using a melon baller, scoop out half of the interior of the cucumber slices. Arrange on a platter.

In a food processor, combine the cream cheese, salmon, and dill until smooth.

Fill the interior of the cucumber with a dollop of the smoked salmon mixture and top with a sprig of dill.

Serve immediately.

blueberry mini-tarts

Makes 1 dozen tarts

These are beyond simple, and if you buy the phyllo dough cups already made, they get even easier. Just be sure to make enough because they go fast!

1 package phyllo dough, defrosted
4 ounces cream cheese, softened
1/4 cup sour cream
1 tablespoon lemon zest
1 teaspoon vanilla
1 cup fresh blueberries

Preheat the oven to 325°.

Lay phyllo dough out on a cutting board and cut circles out using a 2" diameter biscuit cutter. Press dough circles into a mini muffin tin to form cups. Bake 8 to 10 minutes or until lightly golden brown on the edges. Let cool completely.

In a stand mixer, combine cream cheese, sour cream, zest, and vanilla until smooth. Fill a pastry bag, fitted with an Ateco #9 decorating tube, with the cream cheese mixture. Pipe about 1/2 tablespoon of cream cheese mixture into each phyllo cup, or until the cup is a little more than half full. Top each cup with 3 fresh blueberries.

marionberry martini

You can find marionberry syrup in the grocery aisle next to the pancake syrup. It's not hard to make your own either. And it makes a lovely, simple cocktail.

2 cups marionberries (or half raspberries and half blackberries if marionberries are not available)
1/2 cup sugar
1/2 cup water
2 cups berry vodka
fresh berries for serving

In a small saucepan, simmer together berries, sugar, and water. Let cook for about 1/2 hour, slightly mashing the berries as they cook. When sugar has dissolved and berries have cooked out some of their juice, place in a blender and purée until smooth.

Pour puréed berry mixture into a pitcher and stir in berry vodka. Add ice and serve immediately. An alternative is to add 1 shot of berry mixture and 1 shot of vodka into a cocktail shaker and mix over ice.

Serve in a martini glass garnished with a fresh berry.

shell wine glass name tags

Makes 1 tag

Finding your glass in a crowd is always a problem. There are all kinds of ready-made tags you can buy, but then you have to remember what color you are! These name tags are simple to make and personalizing them for every guest adds a special touch to any event.

1 small (1") shell
paint pen
hot glue gun
8" of ribbon

step 1 :: Write a guest's name on the inside of the shell using the paint pen.

step 2 :: Apply a dab of hot glue to the back of the shell and attach the center of the ribbon length to the glue. Let dry.

step 3 :: Tie the ends of the ribbon around the stem of the glass.

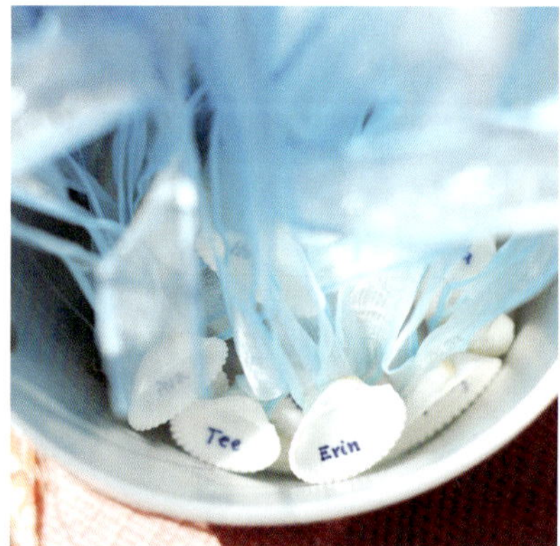

Mackenzie

poolside lunch
for young ladies

menu

::

ahi poke bites

mccarthy-esque chopped salad

roasted plums

faux bellini

When my cousin Victoria turned 16 it only seemed appropriate that the famous Beverly Hills Hotel serve as the inspiration for this glamorous girls' party.

A house with a pool was perfect for this kind of party, as nearly every party in L.A. seems to revolve around a clear blue pool. The pool at the Beverly Hills Hotel is surrounded by big white lounge chairs, pink stripes, and urns full of lemons. It's stunningly beautiful, simple, feminine, and easy to replicate for your own party.

I used white terry cloth lawn chairs, pink striped beach towels, and white canvas umbrellas to create my own poolside cabanas for the girls to lounge on as they swam and tanned by the pool. While they enjoyed the beautiful sunny day, I served them a signature drink from the golden age of film—the Bellini. But since the girls were only sixteen, I adjusted the recipe to create the perfect peach-y Faux Bellini.

For lunch, the menu from the Polo Lounge at the Beverly Hills Hotel was the inspiration. Since I didn't have exact recipes from the hotel, I made my version of their famous McCarthy salad. I created a chopped salad topped with some of my favorite things including hardboiled eggs, beets, chicken, and cheese—with dressing on the side, trés L.A.

Creating a Beverly Hills inspired table was really simple. I topped our poolside table with an oversized pink and white striped beach towel, a pile of fresh lemons, and pink and white polka-dot napkins. Tucked in with the lemons, I used papier-mâché orchids that I picked up on a trip to Hawaii. Fresh orchids, hibiscus, or pink roses would look beautiful as well.

Get inspired by your favorite spot and use their colors to make your party reflect the location.

Be sure to have **sunscreen** and **extra sunglasses** available for sunbathing beauties.

I made **invitations** using a font similar to the **signature font** from the Beverly Hills Hotel. It's a simple way to customize an invitation.

ahi poke bites

Serves 4 to 6

Poke (po-kay) is a Hawaiian specialty and every family has its own way of making it. My way attempts to recreate my favorite poke on the island—I think it may even surpass it! Be sure to start with the best fish you can find.

1/2 pound sashimi grade tuna
2 tablespoons soy sauce
2 tablespoons sesame oil
1/2 teaspoon fish sauce
1 clove garlic, finely chopped
2 scallions, finely chopped

Dice tuna into bite-sized pieces and toss with all ingredients. Marinade overnight in the refrigerator and serve cold. Remember to get the highest grade fish you can because you are serving it raw.

mccarthy-esque chopped salad

Serves 4

The signature salad at the Polo Lounge in the Beverly Hills Hotel is the McCarthy Salad. It's really good—and really easy. I simplified it by making everything chopped evenly and tossed together.

1 large head butter lettuce, divided into 4 parts
2 cups cooked and diced chicken breast
2 cups cherry tomatoes, sliced in half
4 slices bacon, cooked and crumbled
2 hardboiled eggs, sliced
1 large red beet, cooked and diced
1/2 cup cheddar cheese, diced
blue cheese dressing

Arrange lettuce on 4 small plates. In a large bowl, toss together all ingredients except the beets.

Divide the salad mixture evenly among the 4 plates. Sprinkle the tops with beets. Serve with blue cheese dressing on the side.

roasted plums

Serves 4

Cut 4 plums in half and remove the pits. Roast in the oven at 400° for 10 minutes or until the middles begin to bubble and the sugars from the fruit rise to the top and brown. If your plums aren't quite ripe, sprinkle sugar over the tops. Watch them carefully—they can burn!

Serve with fresh whipped cream or vanilla ice cream.

faux bellini

3 very ripe peaches
sugar
water
sparkling cider
peach slices for garnish

Peel and pit the peaches and throw them in the blender. Blend until completely smooth. The peach mixture should be thick, but pour-able. If peaches are too thick, add a splash of water to thin out. If they are not sweet enough for your taste, add a little sugar to the blender.

In the bottom of a champagne glass, pour 1 ounce of peach purée. Top the glass with sparkling cider and a sliver of fresh peach.

a lovely (long island) iced tea party

menu

::

chilled cucumber soup

ladies tea sandwiches

shortbread

strawberry jam cake

long island iced tea

craft

::

homemade blueberry jam

In the spring, as the sun comes out and the flowers start to bloom, I like to invite my girlfriends over for a modern day tea party on the lawn to celebrate the end of the dreary winter days. My advice is to skip the frou frou sandwiches and delicate cups of tea. I serve something hearty and inviting—something that all mommies in the afternoon might desperately need.

As my girlfriends arrive, I serve Long Island Iced Tea (it is a tea party, after all) and lead them out to the garden for the celebration. I set the table with a floral extravaganza of floral tablecloths, floral china, antique floral tea cups, and floral centerpieces. I have an abundance of flower covered dishes and china from my grandmother's collection. If your grandmother wasn't an avid china collector like mine was, try thrift stores and yard sales to build your own collection.

Modern day tea sandwiches and lots of cookies provide the perfect lunch to gossip over. I update all of my favorite flavors from a traditional afternoon tea and make them my own: cucumber sandwiches become cucumber soup, miniature tea sandwiches are stacked high with fabulous fillings, and dessert is a plate piled with cookies of all kinds. A selection of teas, iced and alcoholic, gives everyone a chance to find their favorite—and indulge a little bit mid-day.

Pile all of your **tea sandwiches** on tiered platters and you won't have to refill them mid-party.

If you're serving outdoors, bring **vintage umbrellas** so that your delicate guests can **shade themselves** from the midday sun.

Make a batch of **homemade blueberry jam** to serve at the tea party and reserve a few jars to send home with your guests

chilled cucumber soup

Serves 4

2 medium cucumbers, peeled, seeded, and diced
2 tablespoons butter
1/2 yellow onion, diced
4 cups chicken stock
2 tablespoons chopped dill
1/2 cup plain yogurt
salt and pepper
dill sprigs for garnish
cucumber slices for garnish

Sprinkle cucumber with about 1 tablespoon of salt and set aside.

In a medium saucepan, melt the butter and sauté the onions until translucent. Add stock and dill to the onions and bring to a boil. Rinse the cucumbers off and add them to the saucepan. Cook for about 5 minutes. Cool slightly and purée with a food mill. Taste the soup and season with salt and pepper, as needed.

Refrigerate until ready to use. When ready to serve, stir in yogurt and garnish with a sprig of dill or a slice of cucumber.

ladies tea sandwiches

green apple ham :: Slice a baguette into 1" rounds, spread 1 tablespoon of brie on each slice and top with a small slice of ham and a sliver of green apple.

grilled chicken parmesan :: Slice a loaf of hearty Italian bread into small rounds and preheat the broiler. Slice cooked chicken breast and place several pieces on top of half the rounds and sprinkle with parmesan cheese. Place the chicken-topped rounds on a cookie sheet and broil until the cheese begins to bubble. Pull out of the oven and top immediately with remaining slices of bread. Serve warm.

roasted vegetable & feta :: Preheat the oven to 350°. Slice eggplant, red bell pepper, onions, and zucchini into thin slices. Place vegetables on a roasting pan and drizzle with olive oil until just coated. Roast in the oven for 10 minutes or until all pieces are slightly browned and softened. In a food processor, blend together feta cheese with heavy cream. Spread 1 tablespoon feta blend on each slice of bread and top with 1 of each vegetable.

smoked salmon dill :: In a food processor, blend together cream cheese with dill until smooth. Spread 1 tablespoon of the cream cheese mixture on a slice of bread and top with a slice of smoked salmon and a sprig of dill.

shortbread

Shortbread is a perfect base for almost any kind of topping and is also decadently buttery just by itself. I love it with a little coffee in the morning or tea in the afternoon. It is such a simple recipe to make, there's almost no excuse for not making your own.

1 1/4 cups flour
3 tablespoons cornstarch
1/2 cup butter, softened
1/4 cup powdered sugar
2 tablespoons sugar, divided

Preheat the oven to 375°.

Combine the flour and cornstarch in a bowl and set aside. Cream together butter, powdered sugar, and 1 tablespoon sugar until well blended. Add flour mixture and blend until completely blended. Mixture will be a little crumbly and sandy.

Press the mixture firmly into the bottom of a springform pan. Use the bottom of a glass cup to ensure the mixture is even and smooth. Score the dough into wedges like a pizza and prick each wedge with the tines of a fork. Sprinkle with the remaining tablespoon of sugar and bake 25 minutes until lightly golden brown.

Remove from the oven and let cool slightly. Cut along score lines with a sharp chef's knife before shortbread is completely cooled.

strawberry jam cake

I saw a recipe for a cake that contained jam and I knew I had to try it. But the cake recipe I tried turned out dry and overly sweet. I became so focused on finding a good recipe for a "jam cake" that I started from scratch until I finally landed on the perfect recipe. I've used every kind of jam imaginable for this cake and have found that homemade strawberry jam is my favorite.

3 cups flour
1 tablespoon baking powder
I cup unsalted butter, melted
2 cups sugar
1 teaspoon vanilla
4 eggs
1 cup strawberry jam

Preheat the oven to 350°.

Grease the bottom (not the sides) of two 9" round pans. In a small bowl, whisk together flour and baking powder and set aside.

In a large mixing bowl, beat together the butter and sugar until smooth. Add the vanilla until incorporated. Add eggs, one at a time, beating well after each one is added. With the mixer on medium speed, add the flour and the jam alternately beginning and ending with flour until both are fully incorporated.

Divide the batter between the pans and bake about 30 minutes, until a toothpick inserted in the cake comes out clean.

Frost with your favorite butter cream frosting.

BE WELL RED™ TEAS
get what you need
get
get a grip
HERB TEA FOR PMS/MENOPAUSE

long island iced tea

These are dangerous. I recommend having one—small one—and then switching to something with less alcohol. This is basically a liqueur cabinet graveyard.

1 part vodka
1 part tequila
1 part rum
1 part gin
1 part triple sec
1 1/2 parts sours
Coke

Mix all together and top with a splash of Coke.

homemade blueberry jam

This is my favorite, hands down. One batch never seems to last long enough for me, but it gives me something to look forward to making at the end of every summer.

4 cups crushed blueberries
2 cups sugar
1 tablespoon butter

In a small pan, heat 2 cups of water over very low heat. Drop the metal canning lids in to soften the rubber edges.

Combine berries and sugar in a thick bottomed sauce pan. (Be sure to use a wide bottomed pan.) Stir over medium-low heat for 3 minutes or until sugar is dissolved. Add the butter and turn up the heat to a rapid boil. Stir constantly, trying not to damage the berries too much, until the jam is thick. To test, drop a tablespoon of mixture onto a plate. If it's the right consistency, it will stay in place.

Pour the jam into hot sterilized jars and seal immediately with metal rings and lids.

family picnic
at the park

menu

::

baked fried chicken

roasted potato salad

chocolate peanut butter bars

oatmeal raisin cookies

rainier cherry lemonade

crafts

::

raspberry jam

homemade pickles

picnic blanket

A picnic in the park is an iconic element every summer—it's also one of my favorite ways to entertain. Hosting a picnic at the park keeps everything laid back and simple because kids can run around and play while adults hang out on picnic blankets and catch up. The food is equally as simple.

A picnic menu is pretty standard fare, so it relieves the pressure of menu planning and allows a really good classic recipe to shine through. Combined with the flavors of the season and a lot of dessert, you know you're in for a good time.

In a bucolic setting like a park, vintage only seems appropriate. I chose oilcloth for the tablecloth, both for it's nostalgia and durability. Oilcloth doesn't fray when cut (you can bring it straight from the fabric store and trim it on-site) and it wipes clean with a wet sponge—perfect for a picnic table! My collection of vintage scarves became liners for baskets that held cookies and rolls.

My homemade pickles and jams weren't just great condiments on the table, but were packaged up to send home with everyone. If you've ever made jam before, you know that having willing recipients is a necessary part of jam making. I always end up with WAY more than we can eat. If you haven't made jam before—you should! It's simple and delicious.

Don't forget something to sit on. I've created the perfect blanket for picnics—oilcloth on one side for durability and poodle chenille on the other for coziness.

Freeze **watermelon cubes** and use them as ice in a pitcher of water.

Make **paper pinwheels** to mark your party spot for guests to easily find.

Preserve your summer bounty by making **homemade pickles** and **raspberry jam** and serve them at your picnic on a cozy **picnic blanket.**

baked fried chicken

Serves 8 to 10

By frying the chicken quickly then baking it the rest of the way, I found I can have all the chicken cooked at the same time plus have the frying mess cleaned up by the time it's done. This is just as good hot as it is cold, maybe even better.

3 pounds bone-in chicken pieces
2 pints buttermilk
1/2 sweet onion, grated
2 cups all purpose flour
1 tablespoon salt
2 tablespoons pepper
1 tablespoon paprika
vegetable oil

Lay out the chicken pieces in a casserole dish in a single layer. In a small bowl, whisk together buttermilk and grated onion. Pour over the chicken pieces to cover completely. Cover with plastic wrap and refrigerate overnight.

Preheat the oven to 400˚.

Combine flour, salt, pepper and paprika in a bowl. Take the chicken out of the buttermilk one piece at a time, shaking off excess, and dunk them in the flour. Place the floured chicken on a rack until all pieces are coated.

Pour 1" of oil into a heavy bottomed pan. Heat the oil to 350° and use a thermometer to maintain the temperature exactly—it's important. Place several pieces of chicken into the oil at a time. Fry until brown on all sides. Don't add too many pieces at the same time or the pan will cool off too dramatically. The heat needs to remain as close to 350˚ as possible. As pieces brown, remove and place on a cookie sheet.

When all the pieces have been browned, place the cookie sheet in the preheated oven and bake 35 to 40 minutes until there is no more pink inside the chicken and the juices run clear.

roasted potato salad

Serves 6 to 8

I don't like potato salad. I don't believe that anything containing mayonnaise can still be considered a salad. I do like the idea of cold potatoes with fried chicken at a picnic—or really with anything in the summer. This potato salad is the perfect combination of crunchy roasted potatoes and a tangy bright dressing.

2 pounds small red potatoes (2" diameter)
3/4 cup olive oil
salt and pepper
1/4 cup red wine vinegar
2 tablespoons stone ground mustard
3 scallions, whites and greens diced
2 tablespoons chopped dill

Preheat the oven to 400°.

Slice the potatoes in half and remove the eyes. Place on a cookie sheet and toss with 1/4 cup olive oil. Roast in a hot oven for 20 minutes or until a fork can easily slide into the potatoes. Remove from the oven and lightly sprinkle with salt and pepper. Let the potatoes cool completely.

Place all remaining ingredients into a quart jar and shake thoroughly until everything is combined.

Pour the dressing over the cooled potatoes and refrigerate. Let sit at least 20 minutes before serving.

chocolate peanut butter bars

Makes about 16 small squares

Am I a nerd that I prefer my own version of these to Reese's version? Probably. By making them yourself you can adjust the chocolate to make it a dark chocolate version or a decadent milk chocolate version. Every time I make these, they are eaten long before dinner is served.

1/4 cup brown sugar
1 1/3 cups powdered sugar
1 cup crunchy peanut butter
1/4 cup butter
6 ounces semi-sweet chocolate, finely chopped
2 ounces unsweetened chocolate, finely chopped
1 tablespoon butter, cut into cubes

Line the bottom of an 8" x 8" pan with parchment paper and set aside.

Cream together 1/4 cup butter and the sugar until creamy. Add peanut butter and mix until smooth. Press the mixture into the bottom of the pan using the bottom of a glass to create a smooth, compact layer. Place in the refrigerator.

Fill the bottom of a saucepan with 1" water. Bring to a boil. While you are waiting for the water to boil, put the remaining ingredients in a glass bowl that will just fit across the top of the saucepan.

When the water comes to a boil, remove from the heat and place the bowl on top. Quickly stir the chocolate and butter mixture until melted. If it doesn't melt completely, return the pan to the heat and stir the mixture until smooth. Do not let it overheat.

Pull the pan of peanut butter mixture out of the fridge and pour the chocolate mixture on top, smoothing it out with an offset spatula.

Return to the fridge and let set overnight. Cut into 2" x 2" squares to serve.

oatmeal raisin cookies

Makes about 30 cookies

I can't tell you how many recipes I tried to get this one right. It's become a standard in the cookie jar and a family favorite—everyone from my grandfather to my son loves these cookies.

1 cup butter, room temperature
1/2 cup granulated sugar
1 1/2 cups brown sugar, packed
2 large eggs
2 teaspoons vanilla
1 1/2 cups flour
1 teaspoon baking powder
1 teaspoon ground cinnamon
1/2 teaspoon ground cloves
1 1/2 cups old fashioned oats
1 1/2 cups quick cook oats
1 cup raisins

Preheat the oven to 325°.

Cream butter, sugar, and brown sugar together until light and fluffy. The color of the mixture should lighten a few shades from where it started. Stir in the eggs and vanilla until completely incorporated.

In a separate bowl, combine flour, baking powder, and spices. With the mixer running, add the dry ingredients to the butter mixture. Mix until thoroughly combined. Add oatmeal and raisins and mix until just incorporated.

Using a small cookie scoop, drop the dough onto a cookie sheet spaced about 2" apart. Bake 10 to 12 minutes. Remove the pans from the oven and let cool on the pan for 5 to 10 minutes, then transfer to wire rack.

rainier cherry lemonade

2 cups Rainier cherries, pitted
1 cup sugar
1 can frozen lemonade concentrate
1 cup fresh squeezed lemon juice
2 lemons, sliced
ice cubes

In a large pan, mash the cherries with the sugar. Cook over medium heat for 5 to10 minutes until Rainier cherries release their juice and become soft. Remove from the heat and let cool.

In a large drink dispenser, make the lemonade concentrate according to the package directions. Add the cooled cherry mixture and lemon juice. Stir. Float slices of fresh lemon in the lemonade and serve over ice.

raspberry jam

Yields 5 cups

My mom's good friend has a berry farm and every summer we pick more berries than we know what to do with. Jam is the perfect solution, my husband and friends all look forward to it. This recipe is pretty basic, but when done right, it's a taste of summer all year long.

4 cups gently crushed raspberries
3 cups sugar
1 tablespoon butter

In a small pan, heat 2 cups water over very low heat and drop the metal canning lids in to soften the rubber edges.

Combine berries and sugar in a thick bottomed sauce pan. (Be sure to have a wide bottomed pan.) Stir over medium-low heat for 3 minutes or until sugar is dissolved. Add butter and turn up the heat to a rapid boil. Stir constantly (trying not to damage the berries too much) until jam is thick. To test, drop a tablespoon of mixture onto a plate. If it's the right consistency, it will stay in place.

Pour jam into hot sterilized jars and seal immediately with metal rings and lids.

homemade pickles

Yields 24 quart jars

My dad makes these pickles every year. He claims he started making them in college because it impressed the ladies. We still make them every year even though the ladies in his life now are much younger than he is—and related to him.

1 gallon water
1 gallon + 2 cups white vinegar
1 1/2 cups canning salt
1 bushel pickling cucumbers
1 teaspoon sugar
24 cloves
24 cloves of garlic, skinned
120 peppercorns
bunch of dill

In a large stockpot, bring water, vinegar, and salt to a boil.

Pack cucumbers into canning jars tightly, but not so tight that they squish each other. Place 1 clove, 1 clove of garlic, 5 peppercorns, and 1 sprig of dill in each jar.

When the salt has completely dissolved in the vinegar mixture, ladle it into prepared jars leaving 1/2" space at the top. Seal immediately with prepared metal rings and lids.

picnic blanket

2 yards oilcloth
2 yards poodle chenille

step 1 :: With right sides together, sew together fabric leaving a small opening at the bottom.

step 2 :: Turn the blanket right-side-out pulling it through the small opening at the bottom.

step 3 :: Using a needle and thread, stitch the bottom opening up by hand.

football tailgate

menu

::

antipasto sandwiches

marinated vegetables

caramel filled coconut butter cookies

crafts

::

tailgate containers

poster tray

AMH

Husky football has been a part of my fall ritual as long as I have been alive. When my cousin started playing football for the Washington Huskies, I was one year old—and I went to all the games. As a graduate of the University of Washington, Husky tailgating continues to be one of my favorite fall traditions. We park near all our friends, open up the cooler, and spend a few hours before the game catching up.

A tailgate is the last place for fancy food and delicate plates. This is the only time I advocate plastic cups, plates, and silverware—and one of the only times I cover the table with plastic! Food for a tailgate should be just as simple—and in vast quantities. I always make more than I think I'll need and friends passing by always eat it.

Decorating for a tailgate is probably not necessary, but it makes it so much more inviting (and a little less like a 'Boys Club'). I cover our folding tables with a plastic coated fabric in school colors and make UW containers for silverware, napkins, and flowers. I create the non-breakable containers using paint tins from the hardware store, paper, and glue. You can make these for any occasion and they last forever.

Don't forget to wrap up your leftovers before you go into the game. It takes so long to get out of the parking lot, you're better off opening the trunk again and having a few more cookies before you hit the road.

Go Dawgs!

A metal tailgate container is the perfect solution for holding flowers and silverware.

fill a small box with napkins, salt & pepper, bottle openers, and other necessities and leave them in your car. you'll never be without the things you need!

Serving everything on

poster trays

adds a 'fancy' element to any casual event.

antipasto sandwiches

In my search for the perfect tailgate food, I tried cold sandwiches, grilled sandwiches, and everything in-between. Then I discovered that by baking sandwiches in the oven and taking them to the game in a hot/cold bag, I could have the perfect sandwich.

To make your own, purchase baguettes, your favorite pizza toppings, marinated vegetables, and tomatoe sauce.

Preheat the oven to 350°.

Slice the baguette as if cutting into rounds, but do not cut all the way through. Fill every other slice with toppings. I like to use Salumi salami, slices of fresh mozzarella cheese, and diced black olives in one and prociutto, parmesan cheese, and banana peppers in another. Marinated red peppers, grilled eggplant, and fresh tomatoes are fabulous inside too. Don't forget a small amount of homemade pizza sauce in each slice as well.

Wrap the baguette in aluminum foil and bake for 20 minutes, or until the cheese begins to bubble. Immediately transfer wrapped loaves into a hot/cold bag or an empty cooler.

To serve, unwrap the tops of the foil. Instruct your guests to tear off a small sandwich and dig in.

marinated vegetables

Serves 8 to 10

I've had these a dozen times at Pasta and Company—I love them every time—but when I went to replicate the recipe, I wasn't thrilled with the results. Roasting the vegetables adds a ton of character and flavor that really stands out in the vinegar-y marinade.

5 medium carrots, cut into 1/2" rounds
1/2 medium head cauliflower, separated into small pieces
2 red bell peppers, cut into 1" pieces
5 stalks celery, cut into 1" sections
1 cup olive oil
2 teaspoons salt
2 teaspoons fresh ground pepper
2 cups white wine vinegar
4 cloves garlic, 2 minced and 2 whole
1 package frozen artichoke hearts, defrosted

Preheat the oven to 400°.

Toss carrots, cauliflower, celery, and bell peppers in 1/2 cup olive oil and season with one teaspoon each salt and pepper. Pour the mixture onto a rimmed cookie sheet and roast in the oven about 15 minutes until just fork tender. Remove from the oven and let cool.

In a large jar, combine together vinegar, remaining oil, salt, pepper, and minced garlic. (I find shaking it does the trick.) Put the roasted vegetables, artichokes, and remaining garlic into the vinaigrette. Cover and refrigerate overnight.

Serve at room temperature.

caramel filled coconut butter cookies

Makes 1 dozen filled cookies

These cookies started from a newly found love for *Dulce de Leche*. Clearly, I don't have the patience to make anything half that extensive, but these cookies mimic the flavors enough to satiate my craving any time of year. They are a special hit at football games where their creamy centers are perfect against the buttery crunchy cookies. Just the thing everyone needs in the fall.

Cookie:

1 cup butter, room temperature
1 cup sugar
1 cup brown sugar
1 egg
1 teaspoon vanilla
2 cups flour
1 teaspoon baking soda
1/2 teaspoon baking powder
1 cup fine ground coconut

Filling:

2 cups brown sugar
1 cup cream
2 tablespoons butter
1 teaspoon vanilla
1/2 tablespoon meringue powder

Preheat the oven to 350°.

Cream together butter and sugars until lightened. Add in egg and vanilla until just combined.

(continued)

In a separate bowl, blend together the dry ingredients. With the mixer running, slowly add the dry ingredients into the butter/sugar mixture.

Drop small spoonfuls of dough onto a sil-pat or parchment lined cookie sheet, spacing them at least 2" apart.

Bake 10 minutes and allow to cool on a sil-pat. Move to a wire rack and allow to cool completely.

filling :: In a heavy saucepan over low heat, cook brown sugar and cream until the sugar is dissolved. Cover and cook 3 minutes. Uncover the pan, turn heat up slightly, and cook until mixture reaches 238° on a candy thermometer, stirring to avoid sticking. Stir in 2 tablespoons butter and remove from heat. Cool to 110°.

Pour into the bowl of a stand mixer and add vanilla and meringue powder. Beat on high speed for 3 minutes or until thick and creamy.

assembly :: Spread about 1 tablespoon of filling on 1 cookie and sandwich another on top. Repeat until all the cookies are gone.

Allow to set up, and wrap in waxed paper to transport.

tailgate containers

2 1-quart paint cans (new)
1 sheet scrapbook paper
double-stick tape
hot glue gun
school logo patch

step 1 :: Measure the height of each paint can. Cut the paper into 2 strips to wrap around the can.

step 2 :: Place the double-stick tape around the edges of the paper and wrap the paper around the can. Be sure to work from one side and smooth it out as you go.

step 3 :: Apply the logo patch to the front of the can using the hot glue gun.

poster tray

Most small hardware stores will cut glass to order. Check your neighborhood store to ensure they do and take the tray with you when you have the glass cut. It's really simple to check if it fits when you're at the store rather than having to go back to the store in the event it's the wrong size.

1 tray
1 picture or poster
1 piece of glass, cut to fit the inside of the tray

step 1 :: Cut the poster or picture to fit the inside of the tray.

step 2 :: Place the poster in the tray and top with glass.

ISK

pumpkin carving
in the barn

menu

::

sage & pumpkin soup

salted foccacia

salted caramel corn

homemade marshmallows

pumpkin sugar cookies

spiked apple cider

crafts

::

potato stamp invitations

sweater wreath

I love when the leaves change color and pumpkins are in season. It always seems like the perfect time to have friends over to do something fun with the kids—like carving pumpkins. I invited all my friends to meet up at a pumpkin patch right after breakfast, and then to drive on down the road to my in-law's barn for lunch.

Piles of food filled the barn enticing guests to fill up after a long day. We all gathered around the fire pit and relaxed with soup, homemade bread, spiked apple cider, and an array of seasonal desserts.

Creating a warm setting isn't hard this time of year. A stack of Pendleton blankets, hay bales for extra seating, and enough firewood to last the day is all we needed—a little cider certainly helped! To encourage people to bundle up, I had blankets everywhere. I even made them part of the décor and used one as a tablecloth.

To decorate, I found everything I owned that was reminiscent of the fall season and its colors. A stack of brown bowls, orange napkins, and my collection of plates with a giant turkey on them created a lunch service that was entirely 'autumn.' Wooden trays, inherited from my grandmother, were used to hold desserts. To create a focal point above the table, I made a wreath out of strips of old sweaters. The unusual wreath was simple to make and became everyone's favorite *objet d'art*.

I made caramel apples coated in milk chocolate for party favors—my favorite fall treat. To ensure they made it home safely, I wrapped the apples in cellophane and burlap and tied them with an orange ribbon attached to a wooden nametag. For the kids, I made pumpkin-shaped sugar cookies and wrote their names on top in icing.

Keep the kids happy with **apple juice** and **cheese sandwiches** made on focaccia.

Make potato stamp invitations with your kids.

A sweater wreath is a fun focal point for any fall party.

sage & pumpkin soup

Serves 6 to 8

My cousin makes this soup with butternut squash instead of pumpkin, but I like the flavor of the real thing and, since I grow my own pumpkins, there's always more than enough to make gallons of soup.

3 1/2 pound sugar pumpkin
4 tablespoons butter
2 tablespoons olive oil
1 medium onion, diced
2 cloves garlic, diced
2 large sprigs sage
8 cups homemade chicken stock
salt and pepper
1 cup heavy cream
2 egg yolks

Preheat the oven to 400°.

Cut the pumpkin in half and clean out the seeds and guts. Rinse and reserve seeds for roasting later. Place the pumpkin halves on a cookie sheet and drop 1 tablespoon of butter in each half. Roast 20 to 30 minutes until tender when inserted with a fork.

Remove pumpkin from the oven and let cool. In a large stockpot, heat the remaining butter and oil over medium heat, pouring any remaining butter from the pumpkins into the pan.

Add the onion and garlic in the stockpot and cook over low heat for 15 minutes or until soft and translucent. While the onion and garlic are cooking, cut the pumpkin off the rind and dice into 1" cubes. Add the pumpkin, sage, and chicken stock to the pan and bring to a boil. Season with salt and pepper. Reduce the heat and simmer for 1 hour.

Remove the sage leaves and blend the soup with an immersion blender until smooth.

(*continued*)

In a small bowl, whisk together the cream and egg yolks. Add 1/2 cup of warm soup to the egg mixture and whisk in quickly. Return the egg/soup mixture to the stockpot and continue to simmer for 10 minutes or until the soup is slightly thickened.

Ladle into bowls and serve with warm focaccia.

salted focaccia

Makes 1 11" x 17" loaf

I have used a focaccia recipe for years and continually update and make adjustments to the recipe depending on my mood. This recipe is what I'm currently using, and it always turns out fantastic. It's best to serve the day it comes out of the oven, but you can also hold the dough. Just make the recipe through the second rise, cover with plastic wrap, and refrigerate up to 12 hours.

4 1/2 teaspoons active dry yeast (2 packages)
2 cups warm water
1 tablespoon sugar
5 1/2 cups flour
2 teaspoons table salt
1/2 cup olive oil
2 to 3 tablespoons *fleur du sel*

In a bowl, stir together the yeast, water, sugar, and 2 tablespoons of flour. Let sit 10 minutes or until foamy.

In a large bowl, combine 5 cups of flour and the table salt. Make a well in the center. Pour the yeast mixture into the well along with 2 tablespoons of olive oil. Stir with your hands until the mixture just holds together. Flour your hands if the mixture begins to stick.

Turn dough out onto a lightly floured surface and kneed 10 minutes until smooth. Don't stop too early, and add flour only if the dough becomes sticky.

Grease the bottom of a ceramic bowl with 1 tablespoon olive oil and place the dough in the bowl. Flip it around so the dough is completely oiled. Cover the bowl with a dish towel and let sit in a warm place for 40 minutes. Dough should double in size. Punch the dough down and let rise again for 35 minutes or until it's doubled again.

Preheat the oven to 425°.

Grease the bottom of an 11" x 15" large-rimmed cookie sheet with 2 tablespoons olive oil. Turn out dough onto the cookie sheet and press out to fill the pan evenly. Cover with plastic wrap and let rise 15 minutes or until doubled. (At this point, you can refrigerate the dough and hold it until ready to bake. Remove from refrigerator and let warm to room temperature before baking.)

Poke your fingers in the dough to create the signature dimples 1" apart. Drizzle the remaining olive oil over the surface of the dough and sprinkle with *fleur du sel.* Bake 20 minutes until golden brown. Remove from the oven and slide out onto a large cutting board. Slice into squares and serve hot.

For a BLT, top warm focaccia with homemade mayonnaise and slices of heirloom tomatoes, butter lettuce, and strips of bacon.

salted caramel corn

Makes 12 cups

My grandmother made the best caramel corn ever. Then I discovered adding a bit of really good salt adds the perfect counterbalance to all the sugar. It's highly addictive.

12 cups air popped popcorn
1 1/2 cups tightly packed brown sugar
3/4 cup light corn syrup
3/4 cup butter
1/2 teaspoon table salt
1 teaspoon vanilla
1 teaspoon baking soda
1 tablespoon coarse ground *fleur du sel*

Spread popcorn out on a baking sheet lined with a sil-pat or buttered parchment paper. Place sugar, corn syrup, butter, table salt, vanilla, and baking soda in a heavy bottomed sauce pan over medium heat. Bring to a boil, stirring constantly, until sugar dissolves. Once the sugar has completely dissolved, boil for 4 minutes without stirring.

Remove from the heat and pour over the popcorn. Stir quickly to caramelize every kernel. Sprinkle *fleur du sel* over the popcorn.

Place in a safe place at room temperature for 3 hours or until dry. Break into pieces and store in an airtight container for up to 1 week.

salted
caramel
corn

homemade marshmallows

Makes 36 small marshmallows

butter
powdered sugar
4 packets unflavored gelatin
1 1/2 cups water
3 cups sugar
1 cup light corn syrup
1/4 teaspoon salt
1 teaspoon vanilla

Butter the bottom of an 11" x 17" sheet pan and top with parchment paper. Butter the parchment paper and dust with powdered sugar.

In a stand mixer, combine gelatin and 3/4 cup water. Let stand.

In a medium heavy bottomed sauce pan, combine sugar, remaining water, corn syrup, and salt. Slowly bring to a boil over medium heat. Continue to cook until mixture reaches the soft ball stage on a candy thermometer (about 240°).

Turn on the stand mixer and pour in the sugar mixture in a slow steady stream. Leave the mixer running on high speed for 15 minutes until the mixture is light and fluffy.

Blend vanilla into the marshmallow mixture and pour marshmallow onto a prepared pan, smoothing out to the corners. Evenly dust with powdered sugar. Let the marshmallow sit uncovered for 12 hours.

Turn out onto a cutting board dusted with powdered sugar. Butter and dust a knife with powdered sugar. Cut marshmallows into 2" squares and dip each cut edge into powdered sugar.

Store in an airtight container for up to 2 weeks.

pumpkin sugar cookies

Makes 3 dozen 1" cookies

Topped with cream cheese frosting, these cookies are a charming fall treat. I always cut them into pumpkin shapes, it's so appropriate with the lovely pumpkin flavor.

Cookies:

1 1/2 cups flour
1 teaspoon baking powder
1 teaspoon pumpkin pie spice
1/2 cup butter, softened (1 stick)
1 cup powdered sugar
1/4 cup canned pumpkin purée
(not pumpkin pie filling)
1 teaspoon vanilla

Cream cheese icing:

1/2 cup butter, room temperature
8 ounces cream cheese, room temperature
3 1/2 cups confectioners sugar
1 teaspoon vanilla

In a small bowl, blend together flour, baking powder, and spice.

In a stand mixer fitted with the paddle attachment, mix together butter and sugar for 3 minutes until lightened in color and creamy. Add the pumpkin purée and vanilla and mix until incorporated. Pour the dry ingredients into the mixer and slowly blend until just incorporated.

Roll the dough out on a lightly floured sheet of parchment paper until the dough is 1/4" thick. Refrigerate 30 minutes to 1 hour.

Preheat the oven to 325°.

(continued)

Remove the dough from the fridge and use cookie cutters to make pumpkin shapes. Place the cutouts on a sil-pat lined baking sheet about 1" away from each other. Bake 10 to 12 minutes until lightly golden on the edges. Remove the cookies from the oven and cool on a wire rack.

Re-roll the remaining dough into a 1/4" thick sheet and refrigerate again. Repeat the cutting and baking process until all the dough is used.

cream cheese icing :: I found that the traditional royal icing was pretty boring on top of these cookies and not half creamy enough. This icing is awesome on top of the cookies, and holds it shape nicely when piped. If you're saving these longer than an hour or two, refrigerate as the icing is mostly cheese.

Beat together butter, vanilla, and cream cheese until smooth. Add sugar in 1 cup increments until the right texture is achieved. This creates the 'stiff dam' icing for lines and details. To thin out the icing for the 'flood,' mix in 2 tablespoons of whole milk.

spiked apple cider

1 gallon apple juice
1 cup mulling spices
apple brandy
cinammon sticks

In a large saucepan, heat the apple juice. Place mulling spices in a piece of cheese cloth and tie with butcher's string. Drop the spices into the juice and let simmer 1 hour.

To serve, ladle 2 ounces of hot cider into a mug and add 1 ounce of apple brandy.

Serve with cinnamon sticks.

potato stamp invitations

a potato
paring knife
ink pads
5" x 7" paper
envelopes

step 1 :: Cut the potato in half. Draw a pumpkin shape on the inside of one potato half (or have your kids draw it) and carve out the shape using the paring knife.

step 2 :: Use the potato as a stamp and apply ink using the ink pads.

step 3 :: Stamp potato stamp onto paper.

step 4 :: Write out your event information around the stamp and slip into the envelope.

sweater wreath

Last summer when we weeded through our closets we ended up with several sweaters that we just don't wear (a few adorned with moth holes), but I wasn't ready to throw them out. So I found a way to make them into a wreath that's perfect this time of year and always seems to make a fun conversation piece.

fabric scissors
3 large sweaters (or equivalent smaller ones)
wire wreath frame
ribbon
12" length of picture wire

step 1 :: Cut the sweaters into 1" x 4" strips.

step 2 :: Tie the sweater strips to the wire wreath frame. Be sure to squish them in so the frame can hardly hold any more strips.

step 3 :: Tie on a bow. I used a brown wire-edged ribbon because it matched the sweaters.

step 4 :: On the reverse side of your wreath, attach the hanging wire.

step 5 :: Hang and enjoy!

trophy cupcakes
salted caramel corn
pumpkin sugar cookies
carrot cake cookies

halloween
for the family

menu

::

minestrone soup

chili for a crowd

boo beet salad

pumpkin moon pies

gwen's caramels

witches brew martini

craft

::

candy corn balls

In my family, Halloween is just for the kids. They get dressed up and gather candy while we chase them down the street trying to get something healthy in their bellies. Every year we put something on the stove, and every year a big crowd gathers together.

Some visitors are just neighbors stopping by for a quick bite between houses and others are looking for a reason to gossip. The building blocks for a great Halloween night are easy: simple food, festive drinks, and a big pile of dessert.

To decorate the house, I always have something fun to bring the silly spirit of the holiday inside. This year I made centerpieces out of candy corn and used my favorite black candlesticks to add a bit of glamour. Since everyone gathers in the kitchen to eat, I hung a giant "BOO" made out of store bought letters, black spray paint and glitter to hang above the kitchen sink.

Dessert is the best part of any meal—but especially at Halloween. To make it really decadent, I filled pedestals with my favorite fall cookies and candies, then covered them with glass cloches to keep the sneezes off. Set up in the bar niche in the kitchen, the elegant display was so inviting that it only looked beautiful while we took the pictures. As soon as I turned my back, almost everything was eaten. Wonderful desserts are simple to make and the results are totally worth it.

serve food casually in the kitchen so guests can come and eat in-between trick-or-treating.

Keep a large **stack of bowls** on hand in case more guests arrive. And don't forget to **offer soup** to everyone.

Decorate your table with **candy corn balls** to add a bit of whimsy, and a little more candy, to the festivities.

minestrone soup

Serves 8 to 10

For almost every family event, my aunt made minestrone soup. Over the years, I have altered her recipe so much I don't think she would recognize it—but it's still the perfect solution for feeding a big crowd.

2 ounces salt pork
1 onion, diced
5 carrots, diced into cubes
1 tablespoon oregano
1 tablespoon rosemary
12 cups beef broth
1 zucchini, diced into cubes
1 16-ounce can whole peeled tomatoes
1 12-ounce can garbanzo beans
1 bay leaf
parmesan cheese + the rind
2 cups fusilli noodles
salt and pepper

In a large sauce pan, brown the salt pork with onions, carrots, oregano, and rosemary until onions are translucent. Remove the salt pork and add the broth. Bring to a boil. Add zucchini, tomatoes, beans, bay leaf, and the rind of the parmesan cheese. Reduce the heat and let simmer several hours.

When ready to serve, bring the pot to a boil again and add the noodles. Cook until the noodles are done and serve immediately.

Top the soup with grated parmesan cheese.

chili for a crowd

Serves 6 to 8

I have dozens of chili recipes, but this is my favorite for feeding a crowd. You can substitute ground beef to help cut the cost so you can truly feed the masses, but I like a little flaky steak in mine.

3 tablespoons cornmeal
1 tablespoon sugar
1 tablespoon cumin
1/2 tablespoon salt
1/2 tablespoon pepper
1/4 cup chili powder
olive oil
1 medium onion
3 cloves garlic
2 tablespoons butter
1 pound sausage
2 pounds cubed round steak
1 to 2 cups beef broth
2 9-ounce cans tomato sauce
12 ounces Pale Ale beer
1 8-ounce can garbanzo beans
1 8-ounce can kidney beans
1 8-ounce can pinto beans
2 bay leaves

In a small bowl, blend together cornmeal, sugar, cumin, salt, pepper, and chili powder. In a warm pan, cook spice blend with two tablespoons olive oil for 1 or 2 minutes until aromatic.

Add the onions, garlic, and butter to the pan and cook over medium heat until translucent. Add sausage and steak. Cook, turning often, until browned.

(continued)

When sausage is completely cooked and stew meat cubes are browned on all sides, pour in 1 cup beef broth to deglaze the bottom of the pan. Add more if needed to retain some liquid in the pan. Pour in the tomato sauce, beer, beans, and bay leaf and bring to a boil stirring occasionally. Reduce heat to low and simmer about 3 hours, stirring occasionally to prevent sticking, until stew meat is tender and flaky.

When ready to serve, break up stew meat chunks with a fork and season with salt and pepper if needed. Serve with cheese, sour cream, and fresh chopped onions.

boo beet salad

Serves 4

This salad is really, really easy. The trick is in the presentation. You can use beets out of a can, if you must, but beets are really prolific this time of year and are marvelous when roasted. If you prefer not to cut the beets into letters, this is just as delicious when beets are cut into a large dice.

2 large chiogia beets
1/4 cup apple cider vinegar
1/4 cup olive oil
1 teaspoon lemon juice
2 teaspoons Dijon mustard
1/2 teaspoon Worcestershire sauce
1 teaspoon fresh thyme, chopped
1 teaspoon fresh oregano, chopped
2 teaspoons fresh parsley, chopped
5 cups fall greens mix
1/2 cup crumbled feta

Preheat the oven to 400°.

Wrap beets in foil and roast in the oven for about 1 hour. Check for doneness by poking them with a fork. If they are done, the fork will easily slide into the beet. Remove from the oven and immediately begin taking the skin off. The skin is easy to remove with a paper towel. Use several layers of paper towel and rub the skin. It should flake off into the towel. If beets are too hot to handle, wait a few minutes and try again.

In a small bowl, whisk together vinegar, oil, lemon juice, mustard, Worcestershire, and herbs. Set aside until you are ready to dress the salad.

Slice beets into 6 thin slices each. Cut 4 slices into "B" shapes and the remaining 8 into "O" shapes. Toss lettuce mix in dressing and arrange a handful on each plate. Sprinkle with feta cheese and top with one "B" and two "O"s to spell "BOO" across the top of the salad.

pumpkin moon pies

Makes 24 moon pies

A soft pumpkin-flavored cookie topped with marshmallow and coated in chocolate—it's the perfect treat for grown-ups at Halloween. The trick to getting the marshmallow to sit flat on the cookie is to pat the cookie down slightly with a spatula right when they come out of the oven. Creating a flat surface on the cookie goes a long way to creating a perfect shape.

1 cup butter
1 cup sugar
1 cup canned pumpkin
2 eggs
1 teaspoon vanilla
2 cups flour
2 tablespoons baking powder
1 teaspoon baking soda
2 teaspoons cinnamon
1/2 teaspoons nutmeg
1/2 teaspoons ginger
1/2 teaspoon cloves
24 marshmallows, page 146
chocolate sauce, page168

Preheat the oven to 350°.

Cream together the butter and sugar until light and fluffy. Blend in the pumpkin, eggs, and vanilla. Beat until well incorporated.

In a separate bowl, blend together the flour, baking powder, baking soda, and spices. With the mixer on low, slowly add the dry ingredients to the pumpkin batter. Don't over mix!

(continued)

Using a 1 ounce ice cream scoop, scoop the batter and drop onto parchment lined baking sheets. Bake for about 10 minutes. Allow cookies to cool on a rack or on parchment paper.

to assemble :: Place a wire rack over a cookie sheet lined with parchment paper. Place the cookies on the wire rack. Top each one with a marshmallow round. (Cut out marshmallows from the sheet of marshmallow using a biscuit cutter that is the size of the finished cookies.)

Using a large spoon or a small ladle, pour a small amount of chocolate over each marshmallow until all are coated. Remove the wire rack from the cookie sheet. Dip the bottom of each cookie in the chocolate that ran off the tops of the cookies.

Place the finished cookies on parchment lined cookie sheets and refrigerate 2 hours or until the chocolate is completely set.

chocolate coating

16 ounces semi-sweet chocolate
2 tablespoons butter

Over a double boiler, melt the chocolate and butter together until smooth.

gwen's caramels

Makes 24 2" square caramels

My mom usually makes these for Christmas, but they are so delicious I like to make them year 'round. To make them my own, I've added pecans (my favorite) for a little crunch.

1 cup butter
2 1/4 cups brown sugar
pinch of salt
1 cup light corn syrup
15 ounces sweetened condensed milk
1 teaspoon vanilla
1 cup roughly chopped pecans

Grease the bottom of a jelly roll pan and line with parchment paper. Evenly sprinkle the parchment with pecans. Set aside.

Melt butter in a heavy bottomed 3-quart pan. Add brown sugar and salt and stir until mixed. Add corn syrup and milk stirring constantly. Cook over medium heat for 12 to 15 minutes or until a candy thermometer reaches 245˚.

Remove from heat, whisk in vanilla, and pour into a prepared pan. Refrigerate overnight (or eat warm, yum!). To serve, flip the pan upside-down on a large cutting board. Carefully remove parchment and cut with a large, cold chef's knife. If caramel begins to stick, return to fridge and chill.

Wrap 2" squares in strips of waxed paper and drop into a large jar or bowl.

witches brew martini

Black and orange martinis are a festive color—and are surprisingly delicious. They're basically the same beverage. The trick is using black vodka to create two different colors. Blavod is available at most liquor stores. If yours doesn't carry it, ask. They'll often bring in a case for special requests.

ice
2 ounces vodka (Blavod for black martinis or
Absolut Mandarin for orange martinis)
1 ounce pineapple juice
dash of cointreau

In a martini shaker filled with ice, pour in your vodka of choice and pineapple juice. Shake vigorously and strain into a martini glass.

candy corn balls

Makes 1 ball

1 4" styrofoam ball
2 small bags candy corn
styrofoam glue (available at craft stores)
1 clean garden glove (I like the kind with the rubber palms)

Working in concentric circles, glue the candy corn to the ball. When you run out of styrofoam to hold onto, wear the garden glove and very carefully hold the already glued candy corn. If your hands are warm or sweaty, they will melt the candy.

thanksgiving
at the farm

menu

::

spiced popcorn

rosemary roasted nuts

roasted vegetable soup

pomegranate cran-cherry compote

pomegranate rubbed turkey

ali's mashed potatoes

cornbread sausage stuffing

caramel apples

apple cider

craft

::

feather trees

Thanksgiving only comes once a year, but the spirit of the season seems to blanket the entire fall. I often host several Thanksgiving dinners for various groups of friends and family. My in-law's farmhouse is beautiful this time of year and served as the ideal backdrop for a Thanksgiving dinner with my husband's sisters and their kids.

The farmhouse is where all of the grandkids love to play—rain or shine. The potting shed out back, with a wood-burning stove in the corner, was the perfect spot to serve dinner.

In the potting shed, I created a space that felt warm and inviting using cozy textures in orange and brown. The perfect orange wool blanket from Pendleton served as a tablecloth and for a table runner, I chose a piece of brown burlap. Instead of creating one big centerpiece, I created several feather trees and raised them up with candlesticks. Between the trees, I scattered pinecones, mini-pumpkins, and branches of red berries. By keeping the centerpiece skinny, it left room on the table for fabulous place settings and food.

Antiques created a sense of warmth and were in harmony with our surroundings. My mother-in-law has been collecting antiques for years so I had the perfect farm table, benches, and antique chairs already on hand. My grandmother collected old wood trays that were just right for holding my collection of Johnson Brothers "Old Mill" dishes. I used ceramic pumpkins as bowls to hold the soup—the lid kept the soup nice and hot.

Inspired by traditional Thanksgiving food, I served all my favorite Thanksgiving recipes with a little twist. I've found by adding something unexpected to a very traditional dinner, I can create a little interest in a potentially predictable night.

Some of the sunniest days are in the winter when the skies are clear and the wind is crisp. Let your guests know if you are serving outdoors so they can dress accordingly.

Beautiful **feather trees** are an elegant way to create a small centerpiece leaving plenty of room for food.

spiced popcorn

Makes 6 cups

1 tablespoon chili powder
1 teaspoon cumin
1 teaspoon lime zest
1/2 cup unpopped popcorn
4 tablespoons butter

In a small bowl, mix together spices and zest and set aside. In an air popper, pop the popcorn. Toss the hot popcorn with butter to coat completely. Add the spice mixture and toss again until all kernels are evenly coated with butter and spice. Serve hot.

rosemary roasted nuts

Makes 1 pound of nuts

Once we found out my son was allergic to nuts, I had to stop making these. Up until then, I kept them on hand throughout the winter months for a snack or a quick appetizer when friends would stop by.

1 pound mixed nuts
3 sprigs fresh rosemary
2 tablespoons fresh flake salt
fresh ground pepper
3 tablespoons butter, melted
2 tablespoons olive oil

Preheat the oven to 400°.

Mix all ingredients together well and spread onto a cookie sheet. Make sure you only have 1 layer of nuts. If you need more room, grab another cookie sheet. Bake in the oven for 10 to 15 minutes. Watch them carefully, they burn really easily.

adam

roasted vegetable soup

Serves 6 to 8

I roast these vegetables just for the soup. If you want to get two nights out of one recipe, double the number of vegetables you cook. Serve half straight out of the oven as a side dish one night, and make soup out of the remaining vegetables and serve with croutons for dinner on night two!

2 large parsnips, peeled and chopped
2 cups carrots, peeled and chopped
1 medium head of cauliflower, chopped
1/2 yellow onion, chopped
2 cloves garlic, minced
5 tablespoons olive oil
2 tablespoons butter
8 cups chicken stock
salt and pepper

Heat the oven to 425°.

Spread the parsnips, carrots, and cauliflower out on a roasting pan and toss with 3 tablespoons of olive oil until just coated. Place the pan in the oven and cook for 15 to 20 minutes until tender and browned. A fork should easily poke into the vegetables.

While the vegetables are roasting, sauté the onion and garlic in butter and 2 tablespoons olive oil in a large stockpot. When onions become translucent, add the chicken stock to the pan and bring to a boil. Add the roasted vegetables and continue to boil.

In batches, purée the soup in a blender, or use an immersion blender, until the soup is smooth. Return to the stockpot and season with salt and pepper to taste.

Serve hot.

pomegranate cran-cherry compote

Serves 8 to 10

2 cups cranberries (I use frozen)
1/2 cup dried cherries
1 cup water
1/2 cup sugar
1/4 cup pure cherry juice
1/4 cup pomegranate juice

In a small saucepan, bring all ingredients to a boil. Stir constantly while cooking until all sugar is dissolved. Turn heat to low and continue to cook, stirring occasionally, until all liquid is dissolved.

Serve warm over sliced turkey or over warmed brie.

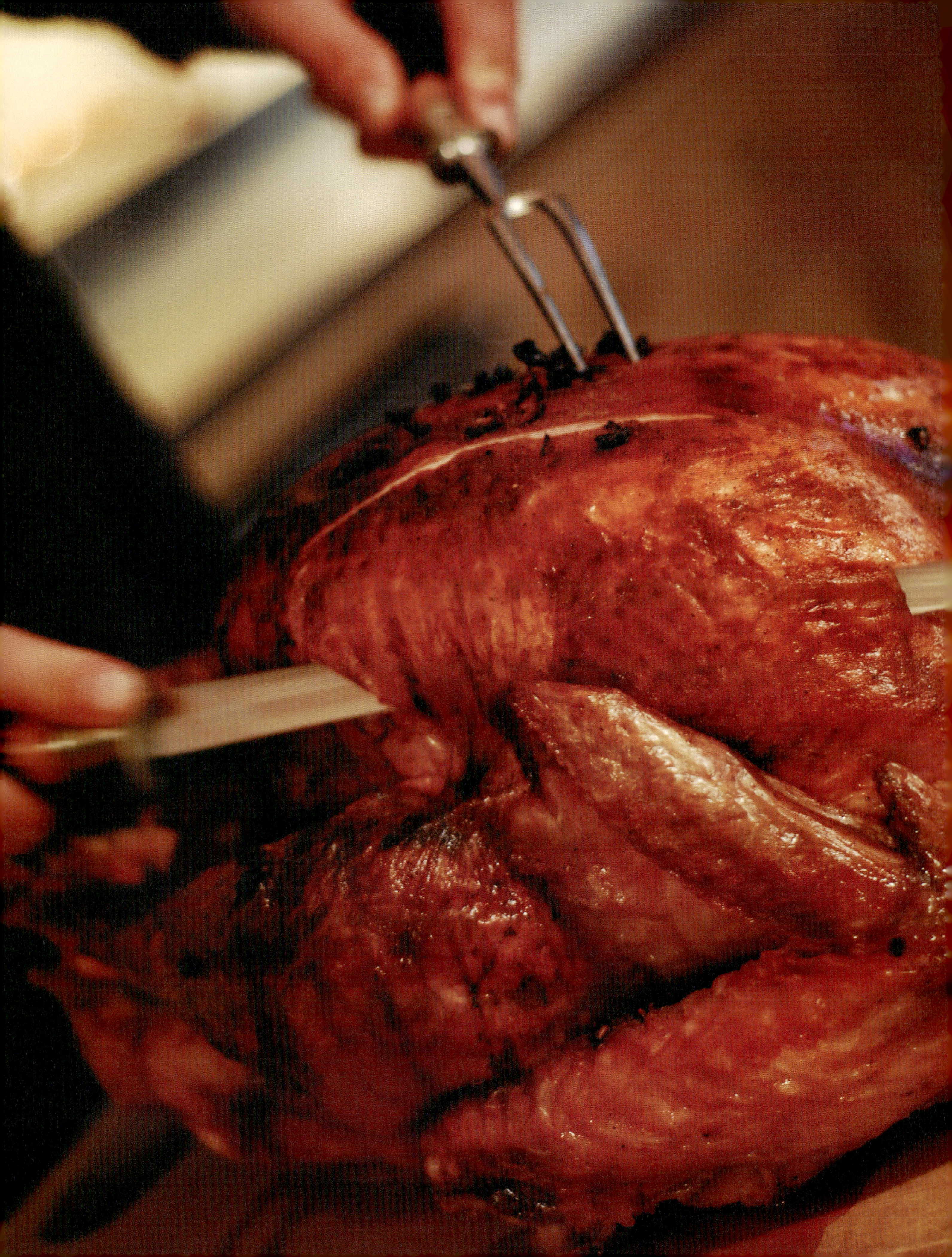

pomegranate rubbed turkey

Serves about 20

1 large turkey (mine was about 20 pounds)
2 large pomegranates
2 large onions, sliced into quarters
1/4 cup dried sage, crumbled
salt and pepper
4 tablespoons butter, cut into 4 pieces

Preheat the oven to 500°.

Unwrap and rinse the turkey (be sure to remove the insides). Pat the turkey dry and place in a roasting pan. Rub 1/2 of one of the pomegranates all over the turkey, coating the skin completely. Be sure to squeeze as you rub so the juice evenly coats the bird.

Slice the second pomegranate into 4 pieces and stuff inside the bird, allowing some of the seeds and juice to squeeze out into the cavity. Place the onion quarters in the turkey, mixing them among the pomegranate pieces. Season the top of the bird with sage and salt and pepper and place in the preheated oven.

Check the turkey every 20 minutes and baste when turkey skin appears dry. Halfway through cooking (when the temperature inside the turkey is about 100°), rub the reserved 1/2 of pomegranate all over the turkey and top the turkey with butter pieces.

Reduce the heat to 400° and continue to cook. Use a thermometer to determine when the turkey is done. Temperature should be 180° when a thermometer is inserted into the thickest part of the thigh.

Remove from the oven, cover with foil, and let rest on a cutting board for 20 minutes. Usually each pound of turkey takes about 15 minutes to cook.

ali's mashed potatoes

Serves 4 to 6

My husband ate mashed potatoes almost every night for months while I tried to find a recipe that was creamy, indulgent, and delicious. It took a while because every recipe I knew and could find contained milk or chicken broth—both water down the texture and detract from the creaminess of the potatoes. I finally discovered that cream cheese created the perfect texture and creaminess to fresh yellow potatoes. They are indulgent, so eater beware!

6 large Yukon Gold potatoes
2 cloves of garlic
8 tablespoons butter
8 ounces cream cheese
1/2 cup parmesan cheese

Peel the potatoes, if you like—at least remove the eyes—and cut them into equal sizes. Place them in a large pot and fill with cold water to cover the potatoes. Put the pot on the stove to boil and drop in both cloves of garlic. Boil gently about 20 minutes until the potatoes are soft all the way through when poked with a fork. Drain the potatoes and return to the pot.

Add butter and mash thoroughly. Add cream cheese and mix thoroughly. It's important to blend the butter BEFORE the cheese to prevent the starches from getting gummy. Stir in parmesan and serve hot!

note :: I mash the garlic in with the potatoes but, if you prefer, remove the garlic cloves before adding the butter and mashing.

cornbread sausage stuffing

Serves 8 to 10

I love this dressing. It's probably not the most traditional cornbread stuffing recipe, but the toasted cornbread adds such a nice sweetness to regular stuffing. I still cook my stuffing in the bird—I like the moistness it creates—but it is not recommended. If you are cooking yours in the bird, decrease the broth to about 1/2 cup.

12 cornbread muffins
4 tablespoons melted butter
salt and pepper
1 tablespoon thyme
1 1/2 pound mild Italian sausage
8 stalks celery, chopped finely
2 medium onions, chopped finely
1 cup dried cranberries
2 cup chicken broth

Preheat the oven to 350°.

Cut muffins into 1" cubes and toss with melted butter, salt, pepper, and thyme. Lay muffins out on a cookie sheet and bake in the oven until lightly toasted. It should take about 20 minutes, but check and rotate often until evenly toasted and lightly browned. Remove and let cool.

In a nonstick skillet, cook the sausage until browned. With a slotted spoon, remove the sausage and place in a large bowl. Pour the fat out of the skillet, leaving about 2 tablespoons in the pan. Add the celery and onion to the fat and cook on medium heat until onions are translucent and celery is wilted. Add the cranberries and cook 5 minutes or until they soften.

Add onion mixture and cornbread to a large bowl and gently stir. As you stir, slowly add the broth so the bread is evenly moist, but not wet.

Cook, covered, for 20 minutes or until heated all the way through.

caramel apples

Makes 6 apples

6 medium size Honeycrisp apples
1 cup butter
2 1/4 cups brown sugar
pinch of salt
1 cup light corn syrup
15 ounces sweetened condensed milk

Line a cookie sheet with parchment paper. Insert a stick into the top of each apple.

In a heavy bottomed 3-quart pan, melt the butter. Add brown sugar and salt and stir until mixed. Add corn syrup and milk stirring constantly. Cook over medium heat until a candy thermometer reaches 250˚.

Tilting the pan, swirl the apples through the caramel until completely coated. Place on a parchment lined cookie sheet and store in a cool place until ready to serve.

apple cider

In Washington State in the fall, fresh pressed apple juice is everywhere! We can find it at the farmer's market, at roadside stands, and even at the grocery store. If you aren't as lucky, pick up a good quality juice made from crisp apples.

1 tablespoon cloves
4 cinnamon sticks
1 gallon fresh pressed apple juice
4 large Honeycrisp apples

Place the spices in a piece of cheesecloth and tie with a piece of butchers twine. In a large saucepan, add the apple juice, the spice packet, and the apples. Simmer for at least 1 hour or until fragrant. The cider can simmer all day long, however, and adds a lovely fall scent to the room. Be sure to remove the spices after 2 hours of cooking or cider will get too astringent.

feather trees

I love fall decorating because brown is my very favorite color. Whenever I can infuse more brown into the house, I get really excited. I saw feather trees at a store recently and they were expensive and not well made. So I bought feathers, styrofoam cones, and hot glue to make my own. They are a bit time consuming (baby naps are the perfect time), but are well worth it. Pack them away well during the summer and they'll last for years.

2 12" tall styrofoam cones
1 large bag turkey feathers
hot glue gun + hot glue
22" copper colored ribbon
2 straight pins

step 1 :: Heat up your glue gun and sort turkey feathers by size. They should be about the same size.

step 2 :: Begin at the top of the cone and glue feathers around the tip covering all of the white styrofoam.

step 3 :: Continue applying feathers around the cone. The bottom tips of each feather should almost touch. Overlap feathers slightly to cover styrofoam completely.

step 4 :: When you reach the bottom of the cone, line up the bottom tips of the feathers with the base of the cone when gluing the final row of feathers.

(continued)

step 5 :: Wrap the ribbon around the bottom of the cone and trim to fit. Apply a thin bead of hot glue to the cone where the ribbon will lay.

step 6 :: To finish the end of the ribbon, turn under the end and secure with a small dot of hot glue and a strait pin.

acknowledgements

None of this would have been possible without an enormous team of people cheering me on. My family, whose support—both financial and emotional—have made my dreams come true: Adam, Lars and Pearl Hedin, Thom, Gwen and Brittney Kroon; my recipe testers and relatives who would take an entire page to list; Jerry Kemp for his initial push; the teams at KOMO, KATU, KIRO, and KCPQ who put me on the air; Josh Dunn, Lisa Patterson, and Ethan Chung who keep me in print; Kirstin Anderson for seeing the potential; and Jeff Hobson, my partner in crime, who makes me look pretty.

There are about one thousand other people who have guided and pushed me along the way. Thank you for believing in me.

index

: :

index

Cookies

Cocktails

Beverages

Crafts